The Collector's Series / Volume 29

NAPKIN MAGIC

by Rena Neff

AMERICAN
★COOKING★
GUILD™

Dedication
To my mother, Leila Reese Cannon, who inspires us all.

Acknowledgments
—Edited by Karen N. Perrino
—Cover by Burwell & Burwell
—Napkin illustrations by Debra Trask
—Chapter heading illustrations by Jim Haynes
—Typesetting and layout by Catharine Hocker

On the cover: Trefoil Napkin Fold, page 22

All Rights Reserved
ISBN 0-942320-36-0
Printed in U.S.A.

More Great Cookbooks!
The American Cooking Guild Collector's Series includes dozens of great cookbooks on specific topics such as seafood, pasta, pizza, chicken or chocolate desserts. For a color brochure of our books, send $1.00 to us at the address below. You will receive a coupon for $1.00 off your first order.

The American Cooking Guild
6-A East Cedar Avenue
Gaithersburg, MD 20877
301-963-0698

TABLE OF CONTENTS

Low Folds

Stand Ups

Children's Napkin Folds

INTRODUCTION

Only limited expertise in napkin folding is needed to create exciting table settings. Most of what I know about napkin folding was learned at my mother's knee. My mother, and hers before her, took great pride in setting a beautiful table. Their accomplishments and reputation were more a matter of ingenuity and personal taste than of money or grand accessories.

Once mother used goldenrod to create a beautiful centerpiece. Despite the compliments, some of the guests sneezed delicately throughout the luncheon.

The other side of the family prided themselves on setting a bountiful table, though the aesthetics were limited. Which was the better approach? It all comes down to personal decisions, but if there is only creamed chicken on waffles or a tuna casserole, an attractively set table makes the occasion festive.

Mother and grandmother knew exactly how things should be done. They may have learned it by studying Emily Post or perusing magazines, but my personal conviction is that it was part of their family folklore, or perhaps a special family gene for entertaining.

Plates were always an inch from the edge of the table. Knife blades pointed resolutely toward the plate from the right-hand side. Forks on the left and spoons on the right were arrayed in order of use from the outside in toward the plate. Water glasses were a scant inch above the point of the knife. (That's all we were taught about glasses as no wine was ever served.) Centerpieces of fresh greens, seasonal flowers or decorative pieces were kept low to promote conversation. No matter how simple the "china", "silver", "crystal" and "linens" everything was scrupulously clean.

Mother believed that it is only after you understand the correct way of doing things that you can successfully opt to do things differently. Otherwise, she warned, people might suspect ignorance or bad manners. (I'm not sure which she considered worse.)

CHOOSING THE RIGHT LINENS

Linens provide the easiest way of varying a table setting. Use ingenuity, imagination and personal taste in selecting napkins and table linens. There are unlimited possibilities.

Look for the unexpected. Crisp woven dish towels can be folded for a clam bake or barbeque. Try colorful bandanas at a picnic. Fold them to hold each guest's knife, fork and spoon. Placemats are acceptable for all but the most formal meals. They come in a wide variety of materials, from country simple to lacy elegance.

A rainbow of colors in solids, prints, stripes, gingham or florals is waiting in fabric shops if you want to make your own napkins, or in specialty shops if you prefer to buy them finished. A few of the folds work best with solid napkins, others with napkins printed on one side. Experiment!

Firmly woven materials such as cotton or linen are the best ones for folding, but some of the folds can be done with good quality paper napkins.

If you aren't sure about a material, experiment. Loosely woven or limp fabrics don't respond well as they won't hold a crease.

CARE AND STORAGE OF LINENS

Lightly starched napkins work best for folding. If you have the room, store ironed napkins flat. This keeps them crease-free and ready for folding. If you must, fold in quarters.

Store ironed tablecloths neatly folded in a dry place. To avoid creases, roll on a cardboard tube or hang on a padded hanger in a spare closet.

For best results, launder linens as soon as possible after use. Pretreat spots, if necessary.

Red wine stains can be removed with club soda. Then soak the soiled linens in soapy water.

Stubborn stains can be attacked with a paste of laundry detergent and a soft toothbrush.

A WORD ABOUT TABLE SETTINGS

Napkins are only one element in creating a beautiful table. When you plan a meal, also keep in mind the following:

The guests: A family brunch should be cheerful and casual. Use colorful china, bright linens and fresh flowers. A dinner party for business associates lends itself to more formality and drama. This is the time to dust off your best china and silver. For a children's party, keep it simple. Buy colorful paper goods and relax.

The season: Plan your table with the season in mind. Lots of candles are cozy in winter, but stifling in summer. Use bright colors for spring and summer, and darker ones for fall and winter. White is always appropriate.

The centerpiece: The centerpiece is often the main decorative element at the table. A bowl of flowers is easy and always appropriate. Be creative and try a centerpiece of scattered flower petals, fruit, nuts, dried flowers, a basket of pinecones, a collection of small baskets or boxes. If you have a flower garden, use it! Even small potted geraniums can be effective. Keep arrangements low so people can see one another and talk easily.

The menu: When planning your table, consider the food you will serve. A hearty casserole will look best on sturdy earthenware dishes. A delicate stuffed chicken breast will look right on your good china.

The china: When selecting china, the most important consideration is your own taste. Whatever you buy should be something you will really use and enjoy. If you don't have a complete set of china, try combining a few sets. It's perfectly okay to serve different courses on different china (it will keep your guests intrigued). If you can't afford new china, scout flea markets or yard sales for a used set in good condition. There are a number of companies that will sell you replacements for broken or missing pieces for many different patterns.

CHINA NEEDS

For each person, you will need:

Service plate (optional)
Dinner plate
Salad/dessert plate
Bread plate
Soup bowl (doubles as cereal bowl)
Cup and saucer
Demitasse cup & saucer (optional)
Footed dessert/appetizer bowl (optional)

For serving, you will need:

1 small platter
1 large platter
3 vegetable bowls
1 or 2 covered casserole dishes
salad bowl set
bread basket
cream and sugar set
salt and pepper set

THE CASUAL PLACE SETTING

Everyday meals call for a simple table setting of a plate, fork, knife, spoon and napkin for each person.

If salad is served before the meal, a salad fork is added. For family-style dining when a salad is served along with the meal, the extra fork is optional.

Dessert forks or spoons can be brought to the table as dessert is served.

THE FORMAL PLACE SETTING

At formal meals, three or more separate courses are served. Utensils are placed from the outside toward the plate, in order of use. A formal meal might include: first course, main course, salad and dessert. (Salad is served after the main course when a first course is part of the menu.)

Set up formal meals with a service plate that is slightly larger than the dinner plate. When diners are seated at the table, place the soup or appetizer on top of the service plate. Clear away both service plate and soup bowl or appetizer plate when the main course is served.

Serve the salad on a plate or in a shallow bowl. The salad can be placed to the left of the forks, or served after the main course.

If you are serving more than three courses, put the dessert utensils horizontally above the plate. Or, bring dessert forks and spoons to the table as you serve dessert.

STANDARD DINNER NAPKIN FOLD

Dinner napkins are large—never less than 18" square. On formal occasions, they are usually 24" square. For formal use, they should match the tablecloth, which may be of linen, damask or one of the easier-care fabrics.

1. Lay napkin flat. Fold in half to form a rectangle.

2. Fold in thirds to form a smaller, vertical rectangle.

3. Place folded napkin in center of service plate.

Variation: If first course will be in place when diners are seated, place napkin to the left of the forks.

Once the meal is completed, the napkin is neatly placed to the left of the plate without refolding.

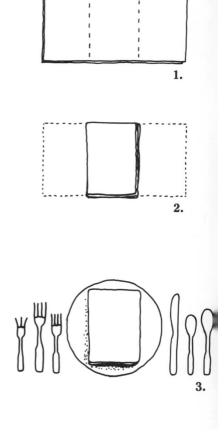

1.

2.

3.

STANDARD LUNCHEON NAPKIN FOLD

Luncheon napkins are smaller than those used for dinner—usually 15" square. They may be presented the same way as dinner napkins, but for breakfast or lunch a triangular fold is often favored.

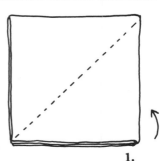

1.

1. Lay napkin flat. Fold into fourths to create a small square.

2. Fold the square in half to form a triangle.

3. Place long side toward plate with open corners away from the plate.

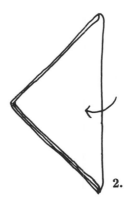

2.

4. Place folded napkin to the left of the forks.

3.

NAPKIN RINGS

In the old days, napkins were used a number of times before being washed. Napkin rings were used by family members to store their napkins between meals.

While that use no longer makes sense, napkin rings are still popular as a decorative element. They provide attractive ways of adding interest and color to a table setting.

Rough, homespun napkins are especially effective in rings. Napkin rings are available in many materials, colors and styles. There are sleek, ultra-modern rings of plastic, traditional rings of metal and old-fashioned wooden rings. You might want to look for odd rings at flea markets or yard sales.

For a different look, try ribbon or lace to tie or gather napkins. Or, pull them through a curtain ring and place a sprig of greenery or a bow on the hanger.

BASIC RING FOLD

This is the standard ring fold. It isn't overly creative, but it is quite easy and practical.

1. Begin with a flat napkin. Fold it in half.

2. Roll napkin up from one end to the other.

3. Pull napkin through the ring.

1.

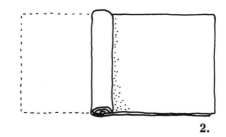

2.

3.

Ring Pleats I

This is a dressy variation on the basic fold. It is guaranteed to make even ordinary meals feel special.

1. Lay napkin flat. Fold in half.

2. Pleat the napkin by folding, accordion style, in half inch pleats.

3. Pull pleated napkin through the ring and spread pleats.

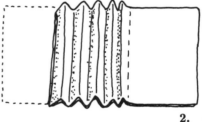

1.

2.

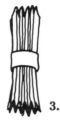

3.

4.

RING PLEATS II

Tuck this fan-like fold through a pretty napkin ring, then sit back and wait for the compliments.

1. Lay napkin flat.

2. Pleat the napkin by folding it, accordion style, in half-inch pleats.

3. Carefully fold pleated napkin in half.

4. Pull bottom 2" of napkin through the ring. Fan out the top of napkin and lay it flat.

Variation: Stand the napkin up, using the napkin ring as its base.

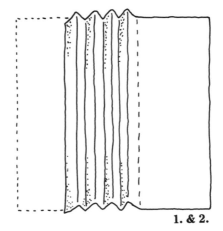

1. & 2.

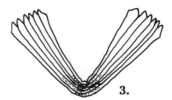

3.

4.

RING DRAPE

Use this drape when you are after a casual yet elegant effect for the table. People will assume you have an artistic flair.

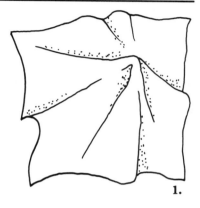

1. **Grasp** the center of the napkin.

2. Pull center through the napkin ring and fluff the top.

1.

3. Lay napkin on the table with the napkin point facing the center of the table.

Variation: Lay napkin ring on the table with the point facing the edge of the table. Fan out the top of napkin to create a flower effect.

2.

CANDLESTICK RING

This neat and precise roll gives a sense of order to the whole meal. When you stand the rolled napkin up using the napkin ring as a base it looks like a candle.

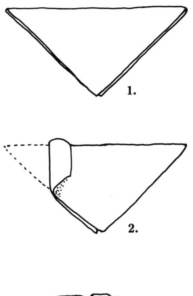

1.

1. Fold napkin from top left to bottom right corner, to form a triangle.

2.

2. Begin rolling from the left tip of triangle, and roll up to form a tube.

3.

3. Pull through a napkin ring, centering the ring on the napkin. Lay flat on the table.

3.

Variation: Stand napkin up in the napkin ring, letting the ring become the base of the "candle."

PALM LEAF

Try this pretty fold when time is short but you still want to impress your guests.

1. Lay the napkin square and fold in half to form a rectangle.

2. Fold top left corner down to center of rectangle bottom. Repeat by folding top right corner down to bottom.

3. Turn napkin over. Grasp top left and top right corners and fold down to bottom edge of napkin.

4. Fold lower left corner up. Repeat with right corner.

5. Carefully pleat the napkin from left to right in one-inch accordion folds. Secure by sliding the bottom into the napkin ring, then spread out leaf.

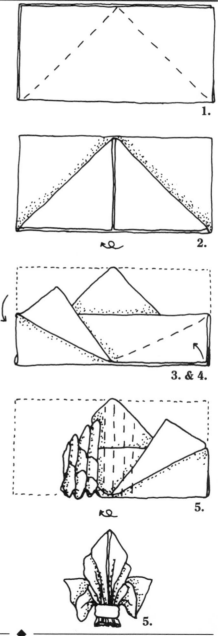

1.

2.

3. & 4.

5.

5.

DOUBLE JAPANESE FAN

This elegant fold can be stuffed into a glass, tied with ribbon or put in your prettiest napkin ring.

1. Lay the napkin flat. Fold in half to form a rectangle, with the opening at the top.

2. Grasp top left and right edges and fold down to the bottom crease. Turn over and fold top left and right edges down to bottom crease again.

3. Pleat napkin, accordion style, in 1" folds. Holding folded edge firmly, reach into each pleat and pull fabric toward you and down.

4. Still holding the bottom, turn folded napkin around and repeat on the other side.

5. To secure, slide into a napkin ring.

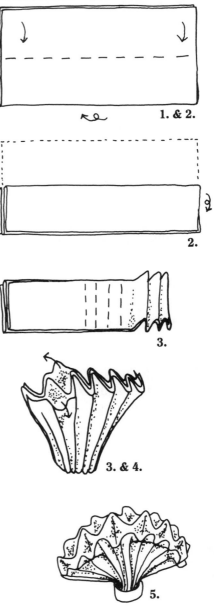

1. & 2.

2.

3.

3. & 4.

5.

TREFOIL

Use a crisp napkin for this graceful fold, which is featured on the cover of *Napkin Magic*.

1. Lay napkin flat, points facing top and bottom. Fold in half from bottom to top.

2. Fold bottom edge toward the top of the triangle, leaving 2-3" between top point and folded edge.

3. Pleat napkin, accordion style, in 1" folds from left to right.

4. Carefully pinch pleats together and insert in a napkin ring. Lay on plate and fan out top and drape edges artistically.

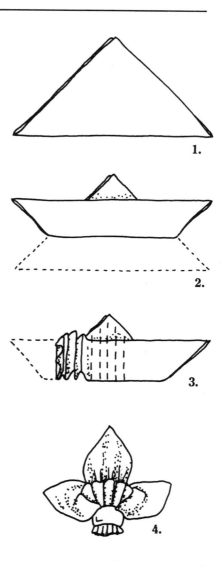

Spiral Roll

This symmetrical fold features points at the top and the bottom.

1. Lay napkin flat. Fold into fourths to make a small square.

2. Rotate the square so that the points of the open side face away from you.

3. Beginning at the bottom, roll the napkin away from you in a neat roll.

4. Insert the rolled napkin into a napkin ring, and center the ring on the napkin.

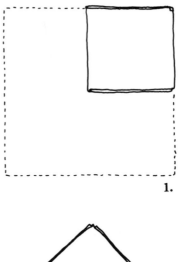

1.

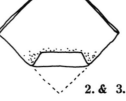

2. & 3.

4.

Bow Tie

Half rolled and half pleated, this informal fold adds a grace note to the breakfast table.

1.

1. Fold napkin in fourths and lay flat, with open sides at top and left.

2. Begin rolling the napkin from the bottom and roll three times (approximately one third of the napkin).

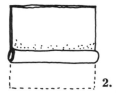
2.

3. Holding the roll in place, make small accordion pleats with the remainder of the napkin.

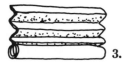
3.

4. Slide the rolled and pleated napkin into the ring. Fan out pleats above the roll to form a bow tie shape.

4.

CALLA LILY

Use this artistic fold to embellish the table at your next formal dinner party.

1. Lay napkin flat. Fold in half to form a rectangle, open edges at the top.

2. Fold in half again, open edge toward the top.

3. Find the center point. Fold top right and top left corners down.

4. Turn napkin over. Roll each flap outward in a tight roll. They will roll up to meet in the middle. Place in napkin ring. Place napkin on dinner plate and adjust the flower petals as needed.

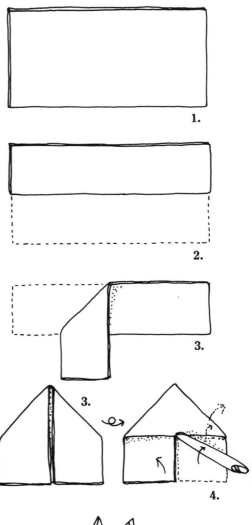

NAPKIN DRAPES

The simplest fold of all isn't really a fold, but a drape. Drapes create a gracious, yet casual look for your table.

Drapes are a lifesaver if it is hot and humid, your napkins are limp and you can't bear the thought of slaving over an ironing board. Your friends won't think you are lazy—just terribly clever.

NAPKIN DRAPE I

This is the "no excuses" drape—with a napkin fold this easy, there is never an excuse for not setting a pretty table.

1. Grasp napkin in the center with your left hand.

2. Use the right hand to run down the napkin and give it some shape.

3. Lay the drape across the plate, or to the left of the plate, next to the forks.

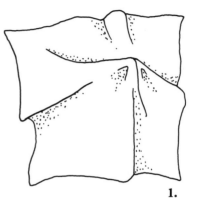

1.

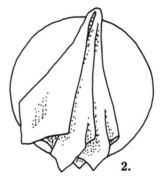

2.

3.

NAPKIN DRAPE II

Here's an easy variation on the drape. It has a slightly more polished look.

1. Fold napkin in half to form a triangle.

2. Fold right side of triangle in toward the center, bringing it just past the center point.

3. Fold left side of triangle in toward the center, bringing it just past the center point.

4. Flip over and place draped napkin on the plate or to the left of forks.

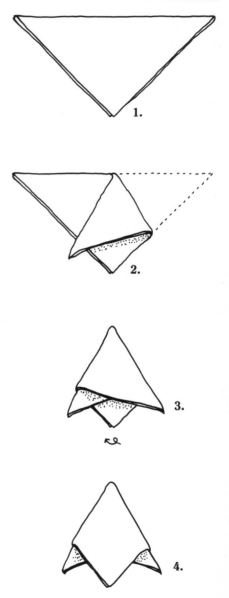

S*TUFFERS*

Stuffers are just what the name implies—napkins stuffed in a glass. Folded or not, stuffed napkins attract the eye by creating some height at the table.

Keep in mind that stuffers affect the way you serve. If you use a stuffer you'll have to wait until diners are seated and remove their napkins from the glasses before beginning to pour water, wine or other beverage.

ABC S*TUFFER*

It's pretty and easy. Use
bright napkins to give
your table an upbeat look.

1. Lay napkin flat and
   grasp in the center.

2. Push the point of the
   napkin, and about a
   third of the fabric,
   into a glass.

3. Fluff the points. . .its
   as simple as ABC.

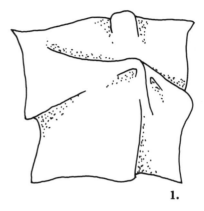

1.

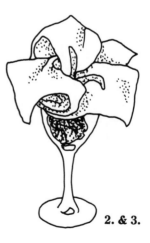

2. & 3.

MONOGRAM FOLD

This stuffer is a beautiful way to show off your monogrammed napkins.

1. Lay napkin flat with monogram face down, points facing top and bottom. Fold napkin in half to make a triangle.

2. If napkin is very large, fold up a cuff at widest point of triangle.

3. Roll napkin from left to right, being sure monogram faces out.

4. Stuff in a goblet with the monogrammed point facing the guest.

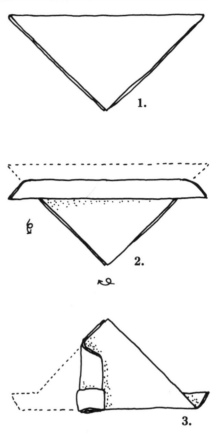

FAN STUFFER

This easy stuffer looks
quite elegant with its
pretty pleats.

1. Lay napkin flat. Pleat
   in half-inch folds
   from left to right.

2. Carefully fold pleated
   napkin in half and
   stuff in goblet.

3. Spread out the pleats
   to form a fan shape.

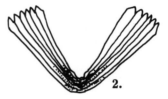

1.

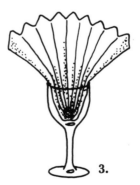

2.

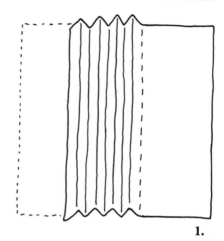

3.

ROLL, FOLD, STUFF IT

This rolled stuffer is so simple that your children can help you prepare the table.

1. Lay napkin flat with points facing top and bottom.

2. Roll napkin from bottom point to the top point.

3. Carefully fold the rolled napkin in half.

4. Stuff into a narrow goblet.

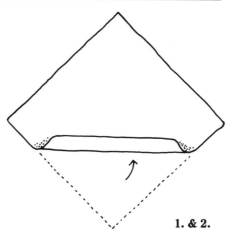

1. & 2.

3.

4.

THE LILY

Like the trumpet-shaped lily, this graceful fold will add romance and beauty to your table.

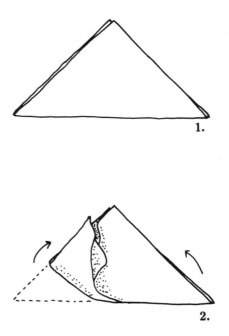

1.

1. Lay napkin flat with points facing top and bottom. Fold in half from bottom to top, forming a triangle.

2. Fold left and right points up to the top of the triangle.

3. Pinch the bottom of the folded square together and stuff in a glass.

2.

4. Drape bottom two points forward and stand third point up. Fluff to create a flower shape.

4.

Fleur-de-Lys

More sophisticated than
the basic lily, the pleats in
this stuffer make it look
quite formal.

1. Lay napkin flat, points
   facing top and
   bottom. Fold in half
   from bottom to top.

2. Fold bottom edge
   toward the top of the
   triangle, leaving 2-3"
   between top point and
   folded edge.

3. Pleat napkin,
   accordion style, in 1"
   folds from left to
   right.

4. Carefully pinch pleats
   together and insert in
   glass. Fan out top and
   drape sides over edges
   of the glass.

Variation: In step 2, fold
bottom edge up to meet
top point, then fold back
on itself to make a 2-3"
cuff. Proceed with steps 3
and 4.

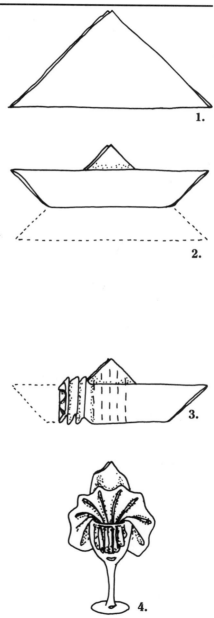

Low Folds

Low folds aren't as showy as their stand-up cousins, but they still add flair to the table.

One advantage of low folds is that they can be folded in advance and stored until needed. If you find yourself throwing dinner parties on short notice, keep a batch of napkins folded and ready for the table.

THE SAIL

A jaunty fold that looks
equally terrific in pastel
linens or bright cotton
napkins.

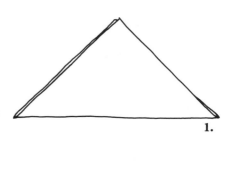

1. Lay napkin flat, points
   facing top and
   bottom. Fold from
   bottom to top.

2. Roll the triangle up
   from widest point to
   tip.

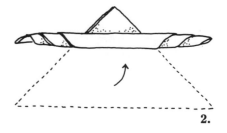

3. Bring tips together,
   place on plate with
   tips facing left or
   right, and adjust the
   point.

Bandana Tie

Try this simple knot for your next tailgate picnic, clam bake or backyard barbeque. Use red and blue bandanas or pretty plaid dishtowels.

1. Lay a bandana or kerchief flat, points facing top and bottom.

2. Roll tightly from bottom up to the top.

3. Tie a loose knot in the center and lay on plate.

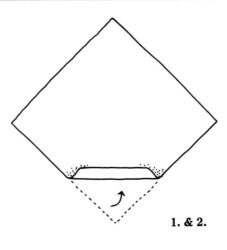

1. & 2.

2.

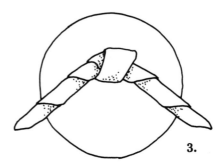

3.

SILVER BUFFET

Stuff silverware in the pocket of this folded napkin for your next buffet meal.

1. Fold napkin in fourths and lay flat, with the four loose points facing top.

2. Take the top two points and fold or roll down 2-3 times to the center of napkin.

3. Flip over. Fold left and right points to center. Flip to front side.

4. Stuff the pocket with silverware, a flower or a place card.

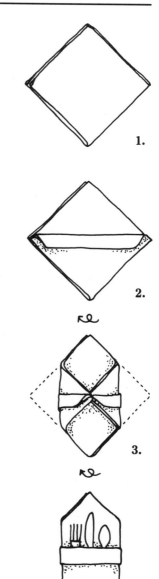

1.

2.

3.

4.

DOUBLE BUFFET

This fold looks complicated, but you will be pleased with the results.

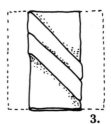

1.

1. Fold napkin in fourths with loose points in the top right corner.

2. Fold top point of napkin toward the center in one inch folds, 3 or 4 times. Fold second point down the same way, 2 or 3 times to create a parallel band.

2.

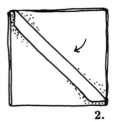

2.

3. Carefully flip napkin over and fold left and right sides into the center. Turn to front side and straighten folds as needed.

3.

Variation: After step 2, turn napkin so the bands run horizontal. Tuck left and right sides under.

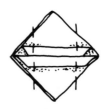

LUNCHEON FOLD

Here is an easy fold for your next spur-of-the moment luncheon party.

1. Fold napkin in fourths with points facing top and bottom.

2. Fold each side in toward the center (not all the way).

3. Turn the napkin over and place it to the left of the plate, with silverware on top.

Variation: for a different look, turn the napkin upside down.

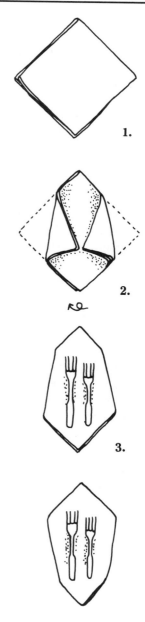

1.

2.

3.

Decorative Corners

Show off your monogrammed or embroidered napkins with this pretty fold.

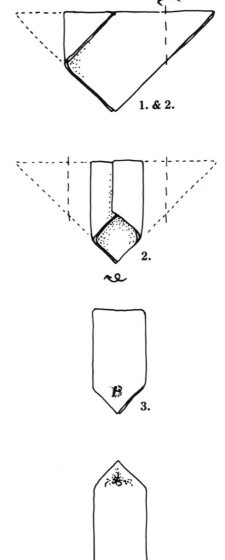

1. & 2.

2.

3.

1. Lay napkin flat, points facing top and bottom. Fold napkin in half from top to bottom.

2. Fold left and right points of triangle in to meet in the center. Fold left and right edges in toward the center a second time, overlapping the edges slightly.

3. Turn napkin over. Place on plate or at left of forks with point down.

Variation: decorated or embroidered napkins could be turned with the point facing up for a different look.

THE TRIAD

Crisp napkins work best for this simple fold.

1. Lay napkin flat. Fold in half with crease across the top.

2. Find center point of the rectangle, and fold from center toward left side, leaving one inch of left edge showing.

3. Finish by folding right edge of napkin toward the fold, leaving one inch showing again.

4. Use your fingers to set in sharp creases.

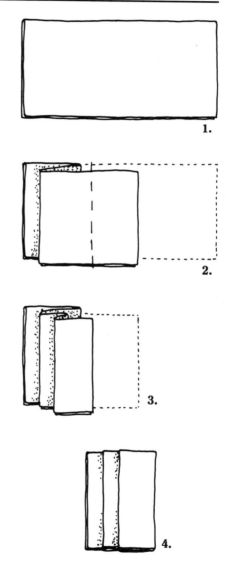

1.

2.

3.

4.

THE TULIP

This simple flower fold looks pretty when placed in the center of a plate.

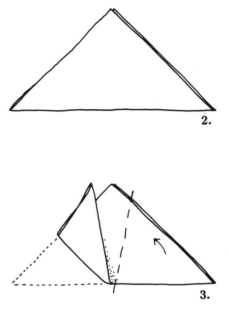

1. Lay napkin flat with points facing top and bottom.

2. Fold in half, with widest part of triangle at the bottom.

3. Fold left corner up to within one inch of center point. Repeat with right corner.

4. Place on plate or to the left of forks. This fold looks best when done with a luncheon-size napkin.

FLOWER POT

Tuck silverware or a flower in the "flower pot" for a different look.

1. Lay napkin flat, with points facing top and bottom.

2. Fold in half from bottom to top.

3. Fold right corner to center of left side. Fold left corner to top edge of the right fold.

4. Fold top layer of the point down to create the flower pot.

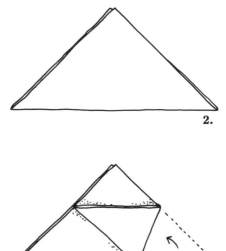

2.

3.

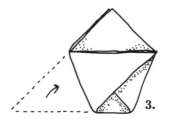

3.

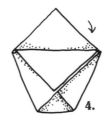

4.

Fan Tan

Use a well-ironed napkin for the best pleats and fan out carefully before placing on table or plate.

1. Lay napkin flat. Pleat in one inch pleats from left to right.

2. Grasp the bottom of pleated napkin and fold one fourth of the napkin up and to the right.

3. Lay napkin on plate or beside forks and spread out the fan.

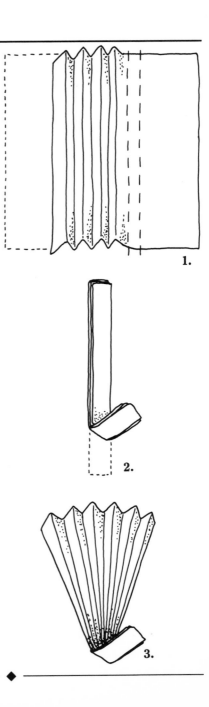

1.

2.

3.

FIVE POINTS

This is a unique fold—and it isn't as hard as it looks!

1. Fold napkin into fourths with open points toward you.

2. Bring the first point up to within one inch of the top.

3. Repeat with remaining three points, leaving one inch between each point.

4. Tuck left and right sides underneath.

Variation: Fold the last point down to hold a sprig of holly or other small item.

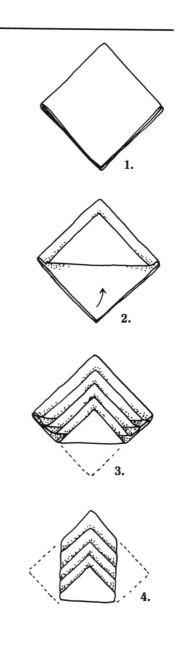

STAND-UPS

Stand-up napkin folds have a formal look, giving an air of dignity to your special occasions. They'll command plenty of attention and more than a few compliments, too.

Use well-ironed napkins for best results. Otherwise, your napkins may flop before meal time.

Bishop's Hat

This classic fold is a favorite of mine. It works best with a large dinner napkin.

1. Lay napkin flat, with points facing top and bottom. Fold in half from bottom to top.

2. Fold left side up to meet the top point. Repeat with the right side.

3. Create a cuff at the bottom by turning up two folds of one inch or two inches each, depending upon size of napkin.

4. Carefully turn folded napkin over. Fold left and right sides in toward the center, tucking left corner into the right side.

5. Turn over and stand napkin up. Pull the two top corners out and down.

Variation: Lay the Bishop's hat flat on the dinner plate for a different look.

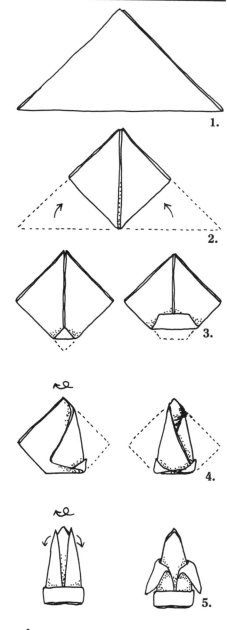

IRIS

This is another pretty flower fold that is bound to be a hit with your guests.

1. Lay napkin flat with corners facing top and bottom. Fold in half from bottom to top.

2. Fold left corner up to meet top point. Repeat with right corner.

3. Fold bottom point up to meet top point, creating a smaller triangle.

4. Fold left and right bottom corners in to the center, tucking one inside the other.

5. Turn napkin over and stand it up. Pull first two points down. Pull remaining two points to the left and right. Voila! You have created a flower.

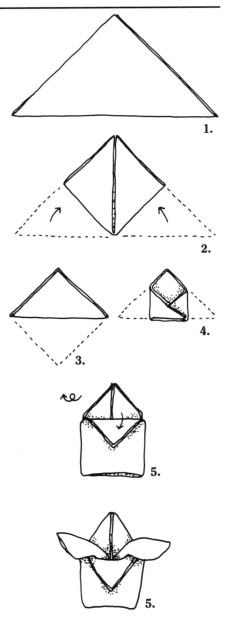

A FAN

This stand-up fan is beautiful. Be sure your napkins are crisp before you fold.

1. Lay napkin square and fold in half vertically.

2. Pleat from top to bottom, accordion style, in one inch pleats. Stop pleating two-thirds of the way down.

3. Fold in half with pleats facing outside. You'll have an unpleated square of fabric hanging down. Fold bottom left point of this square up to the top right, tucking corner into one of the folds.

4. Stand up, turning so triangle is behind the fan. Fold left and right sides down, spreading pleats out evenly.

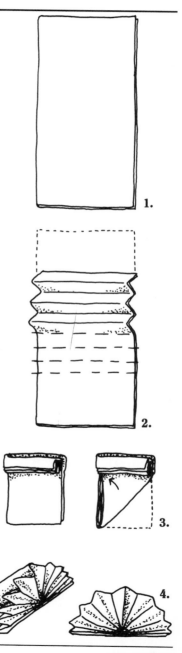

1.

2.

3.

4.

THE LOTUS

Use this fold for a bridesmaid's luncheon or Christmas dinner when you have a tiny wrapped gift for each guest. Place gifts in the center of folded napkins.

1. Lay napkin flat and fold all four corners to meet in the center.

2. Turn four corners in once again.

3. Carefully turn folded napkin over. Fold all four corners to meet in the center once again.

4. Putting your finger on the center to hold in place, reach under each corner and pull out a petal. Shape the flower with your fingers and place a small gift in the center.

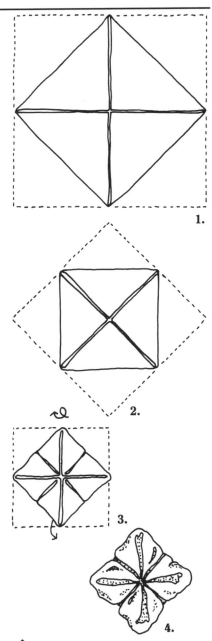

1.

2.

3.

4.

THE SAILBOAT

Use a large, well-starched napkin for best results.

1. Fold napkin into fourths, with open points facing the bottom.

2. Bring the bottom point up to meet the top point, forming a triangle.

3. Fold left point of triangle into the center, with left point dipping down below the bottom edge of napkin. Repeat with right side.

4. Tuck left and right points under napkin, so you have a triangle once again. Now fold the triangle in half and stand it up horizontally, with open edges facing up.

5. Pull each of the four free points up in turn, toward the center to create a jaunty set of sails.

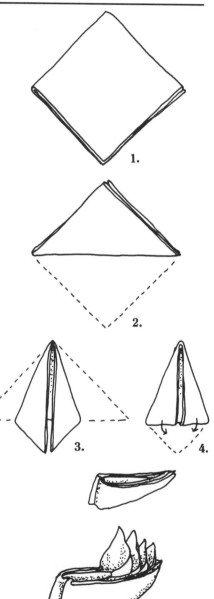

THE SWAN

More difficult, but worth the effort. Use a stiff napkin.

1. Lay napkin flat with points facing top and bottom.

2. Take top corner and fold in toward the middle, stopping at half-way point. Repeat with bottom corner.

3. Fold top edge again to middle. Repeat with bottom edge, again to middle. Repeat with bottom edge.

4. Fold the narrow point on the left side of napkin over to meet the wider point on right.

5. Fold napkin in half horizontally, with swan's head facing you.

6. Pull swan's head to left and bend at the neck.

7. Sit squarely on plate or table and give the head a jaunty angle.

Variation: To use as a centerpiece, line napkin with aluminum foil. Fill swan's back with flowers

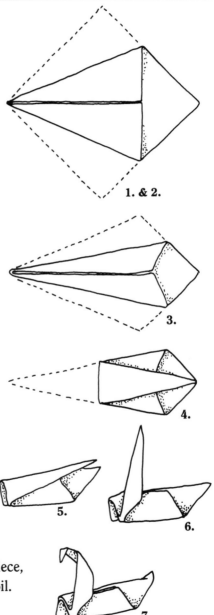

1. & 2.

3.

4.

5.

6.

7.

THE ARTICHOKE

It takes dexterity to create this 12-point fold. Tuck a small favor or gift in the center of the folded napkin, if you like.

1. Lay napkin flat. Place all four points to the center of the napkin.

2. Fold the four outside points to the center of the napkin a second time.

3. Repeat a third time. Then turn the napkin over and fold the four points to the center once more.

4. Holding finger firmly at the center of the napkin, unfold one petal from underneath each corner.

5. Pull out four more of the corners to form more petals.

6. Pull out the next four corners under the petals. You will have 12 points in all. Arrange carefully on each plate.

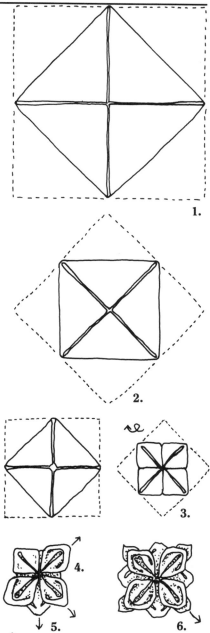

1.

2.

3.

4.

↓ 5.

6.

FAMILY FAVORITE

This simple stand-up fold has long been a favorite in our family.

1. Lay napkin flat, points facing top and bottom. Bring top point down to meet bottom point, forming a triangle.

2. Grasp top left corner of triangle and fold down to meet bottom point. Fold top right corner of triangle down to meet bottom point.

3. Turn napkin over. Fold top point down to meet bottom point of triangle.

4. Fold lower left corner to meet lower right corner (napkin may be stored folded this way). Stand napkin up on dinner plate, tent fashion, with point toward the guest.

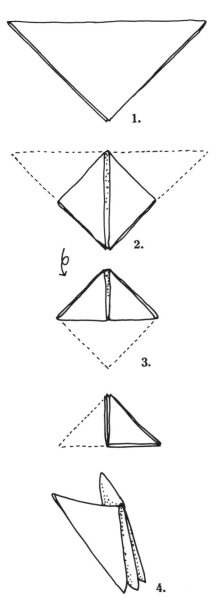

STANDING TRIANGLE

A quick and easy fold for those busy days when you don't have time for more elaborate folds.

1. Lay napkin flat. Fold in half to form a rectangle, with the opening at the top.

2. Fold left side over to the right, to form a square.

3. Bring lower left corner to upper right corner, to form a triangle.

4. Fold triangle in half. When you stand the napkin up, have the open side away from you. Stand up on dinner plate in tent fashion.

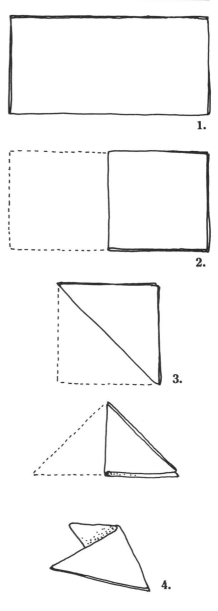

1.

2.

3.

4.

THE CROWN

This regal fold will be the finishing touch to your table.

1. Lay napkin flat. Fold in half to form a rectangle.

2. Grasp upper right corner and fold down to bottom center, forming a triangle.

3. Grasp lower left corner and fold up to meet top center.

4. Turn napkin over, folded side down, longest side toward you.

5. Fold napkin in half lengthwise by bringing napkin toward you, revealing a small triangle on upper right.

6. Tuck right edge into center fold, tucking it into the center flap. Turn napkin over, flipping the right point up and out. Repeat by tucking right edge into center fold. Stand crown up on dinner plate.

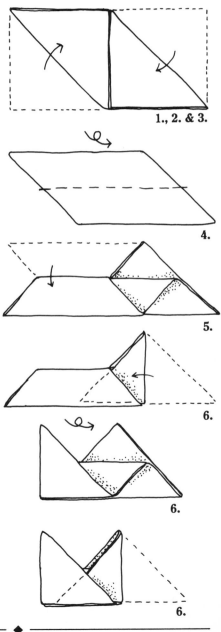

1., 2. & 3.

4.

5.

6.

6.

6.

CHILDREN'S NAPKIN FOLDS

Children appreciate special touches at the table every bit as much as adults—perhaps more so. Surprise your little ones with animal napkin folds at their next birthday or tea party.

On a rainy day, invite your kids to learn these folds. They'll enjoy practicing again and again. If they become adept, let them help fold the napkins for your next grownup party.

Use good quality paper napkins in bold, bright colors for these folds. Use markers to make the eyes, nose and mouth.

KITTEN

Children will purr with delight when you create this kitten for them.

1. Lay napkin flat with points facing top and bottom. Fold in half from top to bottom to form a triangle.

2. Fold from left to right to form a smaller triangle. Turn napkin so the open side of triangle faces up.

3. Fold the "ears" down, and then up.

4. Turn napkin over. Use markers to make the cat's eyes, mouth and whiskers.

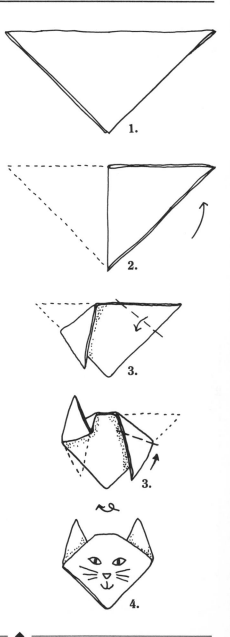

DOG

Use tan napkins when you
create this puppy.

1. Lay napkin flat with
   points facing top and
   bottom. Fold top
   point down to form a
   triangle.

2. Fold from left to right
   to form a smaller
   triangle.

3. Bend ears down. Use
   markers to make the
   dog's eyes, nose and
   mouth.

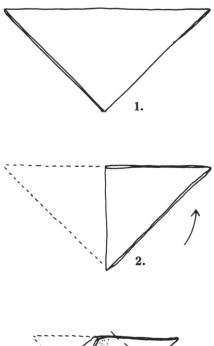

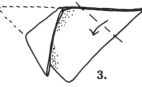

*R*ABBIT

Use a pink or a white napkin for this adorable bunny.

1. Lay napkin flat with points facing top and bottom. Fold bottom point up to meet the top, forming a triangle.

2. Grasp top point and fold it down about 2" and then up 1". Fold top point down again.

3. Fold corners behind and up to form rabbit ears.

4. Use markers to make the eyes, nose and mouth.

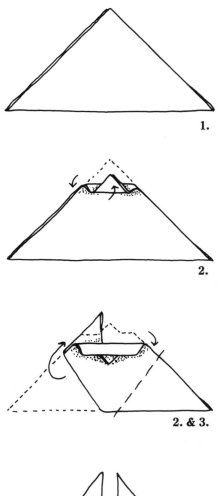

1.

2.

2. & 3.

3.

BUTTERFLY

Use your hands to carefully shape the wings of the butterfly after it is placed on the table.

1. Fold napkin in fourths, then rotate so open points face top.

2. Fold the top two points down to meet bottom of napkin. Turn napkin over.

3. Fold top points down to meet bottom of napkin. Fold in half to form a triangle.

4. Stand napkin up (or drape it over a plastic toy, a hardboiled egg, or a small gift). Use your hands to shape the two wings into a graceful butterly shape.

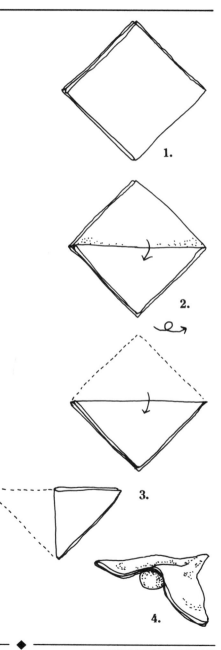

1.

2.

3.

4.

THE CLOWN CAP

This whimsical fold will delight children. Don't be surprised if your youthful guests end up with their napkins on their heads. Works with a large cloth or paper napkin.

1. Lay napkin flat. Fold in half to form a rectangle, with the short side toward you.

2. Fold top of napkin down to form a small square.

3. Roll the napkin to form a cone, with the upper left hand corner at the top point of the hat.

4. Turn up a cuff from bottom of hat, which will hold the cone in place. (The front of the cuff will be taller than the back.) Stand the clown cap on the plate and adjust as needed.

Variation: Flip the points on the front of the cuff down for a different look.

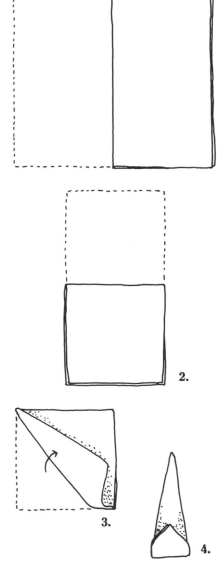

1.

2.

3.

4.